W9-CEG-406

Dealing with Difficult People

HBR EMOTIONAL INTELLIGENCE SERIES

HBR Emotional Intelligence Series

The HBR Emotional Intelligence Series features smart, essential reading on the human side of professional life from the pages of *Harvard Business Review*.

Authentic Leadership

Dealing with Difficult People

Empathy

Happiness

Influence and Persuasion

Leadership Presence

Mindfulness

Purpose, Meaning, and Passion

Resilience

Other books on emotional intelligence from *Harvard Business Review*:

HBR's 10 Must Reads on Emotional Intelligence

HBR Guide to Emotional Intelligence

HBR Everyday Emotional Intelligence

Dealing with Difficult People

HBR EMOTIONAL INTELLIGENCE SERIES

Harvard Business Review Press

Boston, Massachusetts

The web addresses referenced in this book were live and correct at the time of the book's publication but may be subject to change.

Library of Congress Cataloging-in-Publication Data

Title: Dealing with difficult people.
Other titles: HBR emotional intelligence series.
Description: Boston, Massachusetts : Harvard Business Review Press, [2018] | Series: HBR emotional intelligence series
Identifiers: LCCN 2017051988 | ISBN 9781633696082 (pbk. : alk. paper)
Subjects: LCSH: Conflict management. | Problem employees. | Emotional intelligence. | Problem solving. | Work—Psychological aspects.
Classification: LCC HD42 .D43 2018 | DDC 658.3/045—dc23 LC record available at https://lccn.loc.gov/2017051988

The paper used in this publication meets the requirements of the American National Standard for Permanence of Paper for Publications and Documents in Libraries and Archives Z39.48-1992.

Contents

Contents

Dealing with
Difficult People

HBR EMOTIONAL INTELLIGENCE SERIES

1

To Resolve a Conflict, First Decide: Is It Hot or Cold?

By Mark Gerzon

As a leader, you're going to face conflict. It comes with the territory. But before you try to deal with a conflict, you first need to stop and ask yourself the following question:

Is it *hot* or *cold*?

To help you answer this vital question, consider these two definitions:

> *Hot conflict* is when one or more parties are highly emotional and doing one or more of the following: speaking loudly or shouting; being physically aggressive, wild, or

threatening; using language that is incendiary; appearing out of control and potentially explosive.

Cold conflict is when one or more parties seem to be suppressing emotions or are appearing "unemotional" and are doing one or more of the following: muttering under their breath or pursing their lips; being physically with-drawn or controlled; turning away or otherwise deflecting contact; remaining silent or speaking in a tone that is passively aggressive; appearing shut down or somehow frozen.

Neither of these types of conflict is constructive. Conflicts that are warm—that is, already open for discussion but not inflamed with intense hostility—are far more likely to be productive. So if you're deal-ing with cold conflict, you need skills to "warm it up." If you're dealing with hot conflict, you need skills to "cool it down."

Conflict resolution, like cooking, works best at the optimal temperature. If too hot, your conflict may explode, burning your deal or causing your relationship to flame out in anger or overt hostility. Too cold, and your deal may be frozen, not moving forward at all, or the relationship may become icy with unexpressed emotions and withheld concerns. As a leader, you want to bring conflict into a temperature zone where it can become useful and productive.

In the 20 years that I've been dealing with conflict professionally, I've operated in both hot and cold settings. In my work with companies, educational institutions, and faith-based organizations in the United States, I have generally found cold conflict. However, in my work with politicians both in the United States and in conflict zones around the world as a United Nations mediator, I have often dealt with hot conflict. And I've learned firsthand that understanding this hot/cold distinction is a crucial first step before you start trying to act like a mediator in any organization.

Once you've made a definitive hot/cold diagnosis, you'll need to understand what some of the dynamics behind each situation might be.

If the conflict is hot. You don't want to bring participants in a hot conflict together in the same room without setting ground rules that are strong enough to contain the potentially explosive energy. For example, if you are dealing with a conflict between two board members who have already attacked each other verbally, you would set clear ground rules—*and obtain agreement to them*—at the outset of your board meeting before anyone has a chance to speak.

Try this approach: Have everyone sit in a circle, and then ask each person to speak in turn with strict limits (three minutes each, for example). Pick a question for everyone to answer that requires each person to speak about themselves and their own feelings. For example, when I worked with members of the US House of Representatives, the question that opened the retreats I designed was, "How does the way the

House deals with its differences affect you and your family personally?" The result of this sort of question-and-answer session would be an opening round of conversation that avoided personal attacks, allowed everyone to speak, and ideally deepened trust before people entered more-difficult territory.

If the conflict is cold. In a cold conflict situation, you can usually go ahead and bring the participants or stakeholders in the conflict together and engage them in constructive communication. That dialogue, if properly facilitated, should "warm up" the conflict enough so that it can begin to thaw out and start the process of transformation. But you will still need to be vigilant and prepared. Conflict is often cold precisely because so much feeling is being repressed. So you'll need to know how to warm things up without the temperature unexpectedly skyrocketing.

To do this, use debate and dialogue. If a group is avoiding tackling a tough issue, frame the differences as a debate. Then form two (or, if necessary, more) teams, and hold an actual debate. This will accentuate the differences and inspire the group to recognize the conflict that is under the surface.

For both hot and cold conflict. Whether the conflict is hot or cold, the goal is not compromise but rather bridging the divide and innovating new options or solutions. Bridging means creating stronger ties and deeper trust between the former antagonists. Innovating—which is distinct from compromising—means that some new resolution or possibility has emerged.

Conflict resolution isn't something you learn overnight. It takes time, practice, and reflection. If you find yourself in the middle of a conflict and you haven't yet developed the skills to address it, consider bringing in a third party or a professional mediator to help. With that said, if you're reading this in the middle of an intense, immediate conflict that requires urgent action, keep the following advice in mind:

- Make time your ally. Don't rush to act. Unless you're in danger, take stock of your options. Otherwise you might say or do something you regret.

- Determine your goal, and focus on it. Don't get distracted; stick to what matters.

- Avoid name-calling and finger-pointing. Focus on the problem, not the people.

- Beware of self-righteousness. Keep an open mind; you may find that you can learn something of value.

- Listen to everything, but respond selectively. You don't have to address every point—just the ones that make a difference.

- Take stock before you take sides. Don't speak— or take any other action—until you've really heard the other person out. Don't leap to conclusions before you have a firm grasp of the situation at hand.

- Consider calling in a third party. Someone who is not involved in the conflict may be able to provide vital perspective for both parties.

- Allow your adversary to know you. Letting down your guard and letting the other person in may help them understand your point of view.

- Check the temperature gauge. If the conflict is still too hot, don't try to resolve it right away. Agree to come back when things have cooled.

- Observe the golden rule. Do unto others as you would have them do unto you. Be polite. Be compassionate. It may inspire your adversary to do the same.

Keep in mind that showing your ability to navigate conflict is one of the primary ways that you reveal your character as a leader. The best time to learn is when conflict is neither too hot nor too cold. By learning to control the temperature, you make it much more likely that you'll be well positioned to deal creatively with the next conflict that's inevitably coming your way.

MARK GERZON is the author of *Leading Through Conflict: How Successful Leaders Transform Differences into Opportunities* (Harvard Business School Press, 2006) and the president of the Mediators Foundation.

Reprinted from hbr.org, originally published
June 26, 2014 (product #H00VQZ).

2

Taking the Stress Out of Stressful Conversations

By Holly Weeks

W e live by talking. That's just the kind of animal we are. We chatter and tattle and gossip and jest. But sometimes—more often than we'd like—we have stressful conversations, those sensitive exchanges that can hurt or haunt us in ways no other kind of talking does. Stressful conversations are unavoidable in life, and in business they can run the gamut from firing a subordinate to, curiously enough, receiving praise. But whatever the context, stressful conversations differ from other conversations because of the emotional loads they carry. These conversations call up embarrassment, confusion, anxiety, anger, pain, or fear—if not in us, then in our counterparts. Indeed, stressful conversations cause such anxiety that most people simply avoid them. This strategy is not necessarily wrong. One of the first rules of engagement, after all, is to pick your battles. Yet sometimes it can be extremely costly to dodge issues, appease difficult people, and smooth over antagonisms because the fact is that avoidance usually makes a problem or relationship worse.

Since stressful conversations are so common—and so painful—why don't we work harder to improve them? The reason is precisely because our feelings are so enmeshed. When we are not emotionally entangled in an issue, we know that conflict is normal, that it can be resolved—or at least managed. But when feelings get stirred up, most of us are thrown off balance. Like a quarterback who chokes in a tight play, we lose all hope of ever making it to the goal line.

For the past 20 years, I have been teaching classes and conducting workshops at some of the top corporations and universities in the United States on how to communicate during stressful conversations. With classrooms as my laboratory, I have learned that most people feel incapable of talking through sensitive issues. It's as though all our skills go out the window and we can't think usefully about what's happening or what we could do to get good results.

Stressful conversations, though, need not be this way. I have seen that managers can improve difficult conversations unilaterally if they approach them with greater self-awareness, rehearse them in advance, and apply just three proven communication techniques. Don't misunderstand me: There will never be a cookie-cutter approach to stressful conversations. There are too many variables and too much tension, and the interactions between people in difficult situations are always unique. Yet nearly every stressful conversation can be seen as an amalgam of a limited number of basic conversations, each with its own distinct set of problems. In the following pages, we'll explore how you can anticipate and handle those problems. But first, let's look at the three basic stressful conversations that we bump up against most often in the workplace.

"I have bad news for you"

Delivering unpleasant news is usually difficult for both parties. The speaker is often tense, and the listener is apprehensive about where the conversation is headed. Consider David, the director of a nonprofit institution. He was in the uncomfortable position of needing to talk with an ambitious researcher, Jeremy, who had a much higher opinion of his job performance than others in the organization did. The complication for David was that, in the past, Jeremy had received artificially high evaluations. There were several reasons for this. One had to do with the organization's culture: The nonprofit was not a confrontational kind of place. Additionally, Jeremy had tremendous confidence in both his own abilities and the quality of his academic background. Together with his defensive response to even the mildest criticism, this confidence led others—including David—to let slide discussions of weaknesses that were interfering with Jeremy's ability to deliver high-quality work. Jeremy had a cutting sense of humor, for instance, which had offended people inside and outside his unit. No one had ever said anything to him directly, but as time passed, more and more people were reluctant to work with him. Given that Jeremy had received almost no concrete criticism over the years, his biting style was now entrenched and the staff was restive.

In conversations like this, the main challenge is to get off to the right start. If the exchange starts off reasonably well, the rest of it has a good chance of going well. But if the opening goes badly, it threatens to bleed forward into the rest of the conversation. In an effort to be gentle, many people start these conversations on a light note. And that was just what David did, opening with, "How about those Red Sox?"

Naturally Jeremy got the wrong idea about where David was heading; he remained his usual cocky, superior self. Sensing this, David felt he had to take off the velvet gloves. The conversation quickly became brutally honest, and David did almost all the talking. When the monologue was over, Jeremy stared icily at the floor. He got up in stiff silence and left. David was relieved. From his point of view, the interaction had been painful but swift. There was not too much blood on the floor, he observed wryly. But two days later, Jeremy handed in his resignation, taking a lot of institutional memory—and talent—with him.

"What's going on here?"

Often we have stressful conversations thrust upon us. Indeed, some of the worst conversations—especially for people who are conflict averse—are the altogether unexpected ones that break out like crackling summer storms. Suddenly the conversation becomes intensely charged emotionally, and electricity flies in all directions. What's worse, nothing makes sense. We seem to have been drawn into a black cloud of twisted logic and altered sensibilities.

Consider the case of Elizabeth and Rafael. They were team leaders working together on a project for a major consulting firm. It seemed that everything that could have gone wrong on the project had, and the work was badly bogged down. The two consultants were meeting to revise their schedule, given the delays, and to divide up the discouraging tasks for the week ahead. As they talked, Elizabeth wrote and erased on the white board. When she had finished, she looked at Rafael and said matter-of-factly, "Is that it, then?"

Rafael clenched his teeth in frustration. "If you say so," he sniped.

Elizabeth recoiled. She instantly replayed the exchange in her mind but couldn't figure out what had provoked Rafael. His reaction seemed completely disconnected from her comment. The most common reaction of someone in Elizabeth's place is to guiltily defend herself by denying Rafael's unspoken accusation. But Elizabeth was uneasy with confrontation so she tried appeasement. "Rafael," she stammered, "I'm sorry. Is something wrong?"

"Who put you in charge?" he retorted. "Who told you to assign work to me?"

Clearly, Rafael and Elizabeth have just happened into a difficult conversation. Some transgression has occurred, but Elizabeth doesn't know exactly what it is. She feels blindsided—her attempt to expedite the task at hand has clearly been misconstrued. Rafael feels he's been put in a position of inferiority by what he sees as Elizabeth's controlling behavior. Inexplicably, there seem to be more than two people taking part in this conversation, and the invisible parties are creating lots of static. What childhood experience, we may wonder, is causing Elizabeth to assume that Rafael's tension is automatically her fault? And who is influencing Rafael's perception that Elizabeth is taking over? Could it be his father? His wife? It's impossible to tell. At the same time, it's hard for us to escape the feeling that Rafael is overreacting when he challenges Elizabeth about her alleged need to take control.

Elizabeth felt Rafael's resentment like a wave, and she apologized again. "Sorry. How do you want the work divided?" Deferring to Rafael in this way smoothed the strained atmosphere for the time being. But it set a precedent for unequal status that neither Elizabeth nor the company believed was correct. Worse, though Rafael and Elizabeth remained on the same team after their painful exchange, Elizabeth chafed under the status change and three months later transferred out of the project.

"You are attacking me!"

Now let's turn our attention to aggressively stressful conversations, those in which people use all kinds of psychological and rhetorical mechanisms to throw their counterparts off balance, to undermine their positions, even to expose and belittle them. These "thwarting tactics" take many forms—profanity, manipulation, shouting—and not everyone is triggered or stumped by the same ones. The red zone is not the thwarting tactic alone but the pairing of the thwarting tactic with individual vulnerability.

Consider Nick and Karen, two senior managers working at the same level in an IT firm. Karen was leading a presentation to a client, and the information was weak and disorganized. She and the team had not been able to answer even basic questions. The client had been patient, then quiet, then clearly exasperated. When the presentation really started to fall apart, the client put the team on the spot with questions that made them look increasingly inadequate.

On this particular day, Nick was not part of the presenting team; he was simply observing. He was as surprised as the client at Karen's poor performance. After the client left, he asked Karen what happened. She lashed out at him defensively: "You're not my boss, so don't start patronizing me. You always undercut me no matter what I do." Karen continued to shout at Nick, her antagonism palpable. Each time he spoke, she interrupted him with accusations and threats: "I can't wait to see how you like it when people leave you flailing in the wind." Nick tried to remain reasonable, but Karen didn't wind down. "Karen," he said, "pull yourself together. You are twisting every word I say."

Here, Nick's problem is not that Karen is using a panoply of thwarting tactics but that all her tactics—

accusation, distortion, and digression—are aggressive. This raises the stakes considerably. Most of us are vulnerable to aggressive tactics because we don't know whether, or how far, the aggression will escalate. Nick wanted to avoid Karen's aggression, but his insistence on rationality in the face of emotionalism was not working. His cool approach was trumped by Karen's aggressive one. As a result, Nick found himself trapped in the snare of Karen's choosing. In particular, her threats that she would pay him back with the client rattled him. He couldn't tell whether she was just huffing or meant it. He finally turned to the managing director, who grew frustrated and later angry at Nick and Karen for their inability to resolve their problems. In the end, their lack of skill in handling their difficult conversations cost them dearly. Both were passed over for promotion after the company pinned the loss of the client directly on their persistent failure to communicate.

Preparing for a stressful conversation

So how can we prepare for these three basic stressful conversations before they occur? A good start is to
become aware of your own weaknesses to people and
situations. David, Elizabeth, and Nick were unable to
control their counterparts, but their stressful conversations would have gone much better if they had been
more usefully aware of their vulnerabilities. It is important for those who are vulnerable to hostility, for
example, to know how they react to it. Do they with-
draw or escalate? Do they clam up or retaliate? While
one reaction is not better than the other, knowing
how you react in a stressful situation will teach you
a lot about your vulnerabilities, and it can help you
master stressful situations.

Recall Nick's problem. If he had been more self-
aware, he would have known that he acts stubbornly

rational in the face of aggressive outbursts such as Karen's. Nick's choice of a disengaged demeanor gave Karen control over the conversation, but he didn't have to allow Karen—or anyone else—to exploit his vulnerability. In moments of calm self-scrutiny, when he's not entangled in a live stressful conversation, Nick can take time to reflect on his inability to tolerate irrational aggressive outbursts. This self-awareness would free him to prepare himself—not for Karen's unexpected accusations but for his own predictable vulnerability to any sudden assault like hers.

Though it might sound like it, building awareness is not about endless self-analysis. Much of it simply involves making our tacit knowledge about ourselves more explicit. We all know from past experience, for instance, what kinds of conversations and people we handle badly. When you find yourself in a difficult conversation, ask yourself whether this is one of those situations and whether it involves one of those people. For instance, do you bare your teeth when faced with an overbearing competitor? Do you shut down when you feel excluded? Once you know what your danger zones are, you can anticipate your vulnerability and improve your response.

Explicit self-awareness will often help save you from engaging in a conversation in a way that panders to your feelings rather than one that serves your needs. Think back to David, the boss of the nonprofit institution, and Jeremy, his cocky subordinate. Given Jeremy's history, David's conversational game plan—easing in, then when that didn't work, the painful-but-quick bombshell—was doomed. A better approach would have been for David to split the conversation into two parts. In a first meeting, he could have raised the central issues of Jeremy's biting humor and disappointing performance. A second meeting could have been set up for the discussion itself. Handling the situation incrementally would have allowed time for both David and Jeremy to prepare for a two-way conversation instead of one of them delivering a monologue. After all, this wasn't an emergency; David didn't have to exhaust this topic immediately. Indeed, if David had been more self-aware, he might have recognized that the approach he chose was dictated less by Jeremy's character than by his own distaste for conflict.

An excellent way to anticipate specific problems that you may encounter in a stressful conversation is to rehearse with a neutral friend. Pick someone who doesn't have the same communication problems as you. Ideally, the friend should be a good listener, honest but nonjudgmental. Start with content. Just tell your friend what you want to say to your counter-part without worrying about tone or phrasing. Be vicious, be timid, be sarcastically witty, jump around in your argument, but get it out. Now go over it again and think about what you would say if the situation weren't emotionally loaded. Your friend can help you because he or she is not in a flush of emotion over the situation. Write down what you come up with together because if you don't, you'll forget it later.

Now fine-tune the phrasing. When you imagine talking to the counterpart, your phrasing tends to be highly charged—and you can think of only one way to say anything. But when your friend says, "Tell me how you want to say this," an interesting thing happens: Your phrasing is often much better, much more temperate, usable. Remember, you can say what you want to say, you just can't say it *like that*. Also, work on your body language with your friend. You'll both soon be laughing because of the expressions that sneak out unawares—eyebrows skittering up and down, legs wrapped around each other like licorice twists, nervous snickers that will certainly be misinterpreted. (For more on preparing for stressful conversations, see the sidebar "The DNA of Conversation Management.")

31

THE DNA OF CONVERSATION MANAGEMENT

The techniques I have identified for handling stressful conversations all have tucked within them three deceptively simple ingredients that are needed to make stressful conversations succeed. These are clarity, neutrality, and temperance. They are the building blocks of all good communication. Mastering them will multiply your chances of responding well to even the most strained conversation. Let's take a look at each of the components in turn.

Clarity means letting words do the work for us. Avoid euphemisms or talking in circles, and tell people clearly what you mean: "Emily, from your family's point of view, the Somerset Valley Nursing Home would be the best placement for your father. His benefits don't cover it." Unfortunately, delivering clear content when the news is bad is particularly hard to do. Under strained circumstances, we all tend to shy away from clarity because we equate it with brutality. Instead, we say things like, "Well, Dan, we're still not sure yet what's going to happen with this job, but in the future we'll keep our eyes open." This is a roundabout—and terribly misleading—way to inform someone that he didn't get the promotion he was seeking. And in reality, there's nothing inherently brutal about honesty. It is not the content but the delivery of the news that makes it brutal or humane. Ask a surgeon. Ask a priest; ask a cop. If a message is given skillfully—even though the news is bad—the content may still be tolerable. When a senior executive, for example, directly tells a subordinate that "the promotion has gone to someone else," the news is likely to be highly unpleasant, and the appropriate reaction is sadness, anger, and anxiety.

(Continued)

THE DNA OF CONVERSATION MANAGEMENT

But if the content is clear, the listener can better begin to process the information. Indeed, bringing clarity to the content eases the burden for the recipient rather than increases it.

Tone is the nonverbal part of delivery in stressful conversations. It is intonation, facial expressions, and conscious and unconscious body language. Although it's hard to have a neutral tone when overcome by strong feelings, neutrality is the desired norm in crisis communications, including stressful conversations. Consider the classic neutrality of NASA. Regardless of how dire the message, NASA communicates its content in uninflected tones: "Houston, we have a problem." It takes practice to acquire such neutrality. But a neutral tone is the best place to start when a conversation turns stressful.

Temperate phrasing is the final element in this triumvirate of skills. English is a huge language, and there are lots of different ways to say what you need to say. Some of these phrases are temperate, while others will baldly provoke the recipient to dismiss your words—and your content. In the United States, for example, some of the most intemperate phrasing revolves around threats of litigation: "If you don't get a check to me by April 23, I'll be forced to call my lawyer." Phrases like this turn up the heat in all conversations, particularly in strained ones. But remember, we're not in stressful conversations to score points or to create enemies. The goal is to advance the conversation, to hear and be heard accurately, and to have a functional exchange between two people. So the next time you want to snap at someone— "Stop interrupting me!"—try this: "Can you hold on a minute? I want to finish before I lose my train of thought." Temperate phrasing will help you take the strain out of a stressful conversation.

Managing the conversation

While it is important to build awareness and to practice before a stressful conversation, those steps are not
enough. Let's look at what you can do as the conversation unfolds. Consider Elizabeth, the team leader
whose colleague claimed she was usurping control.
She couldn't think well on her feet in confrontational
situations, and she knew it, so she needed a few hip-
pocket phrases—phrases she could recall on the spot
so that she wouldn't have to be silent or invent something on the spur of the moment. Though such a solution sounds simple, most of us don't have a tool kit
of conversational tactics ready at hand. Rectifying
this gap is an essential part of learning how to handle stressful conversations better. We need to learn
communications skills, in the same way that we learn
CPR: well in advance, knowing that when we need
to use them, the situation will be critical and tense.

Here are three proven conversational approaches. The particular wording may not suit your style, and that's fine. The important thing is to understand how the techniques work, and then choose phrasing that is comfortable for you.

Honor thy partner

When David gave negative feedback to Jeremy, it would have been refreshing if he had begun with an admission of regret and some responsibility for his contribution to their shared problem. "Jeremy," he might have said, "the quality of your work has been undercut—in part by the reluctance of your colleagues to risk the edge of your humor by talking problems through with you. I share responsibility for this because I have been reluctant to speak openly about these difficulties with you, whom I like and respect and with whom I have worked a long time." Acknowledging responsibility as a technique—

particularly as an opening—can be effective because it immediately focuses attention, but without provocation, on the difficult things the speaker needs to say and the listener needs to hear.

Is this always a good technique in a difficult conversation? No, because there is never any one good technique. But in this case, it effectively sets the tone for David's discussion with Jeremy. It honors the problems, it honors Jeremy, it honors their relationship, and it honors David's responsibility. Any technique that communicates honor in a stressful conversation— particularly a conversation that will take the counterpart by surprise—is to be highly valued. Indeed, the ability to act with dignity can make or break a stressful conversation. More important, while Jeremy has left the company, he can still do harm by spreading gossip and using his insider's knowledge against the organization. The more intolerable the conversation with David has been, the more Jeremy is likely to want to make the organization pay.

Disarm by restating your intentions

Part of the difficulty in Rafael and Elizabeth's "What's going on here?" conversation is that Rafael's misinterpretation of Elizabeth's words and actions seems to be influenced by instant replays of other stressful conversations that he has had in the past. Elizabeth doesn't want to psychoanalyze Rafael; indeed, exploring Rafael's internal landscape would exacerbate this painful situation. So what can Elizabeth do to defuse the situation unilaterally?

Elizabeth needs a technique that doesn't require her to understand the underlying reasons for Rafael's strong reaction but that helps her handle the situation effectively. "I can see how you took what I said the way you did, Rafael. That wasn't what I meant. Let's go over this list again." I call this the clarification technique, and it's a highly disarming one. Using it, Elizabeth can unilaterally change the confrontation into a point of agreement. Instead of arguing with Rafael about his perceptions, she grants him his perceptions—after all, they're his. Instead of arguing about her intentions, she keeps the responsibility for aligning her words with her intentions. And she goes back into the conversation right where they left off. (For a fuller discussion of the disconnect between what we mean and what we say, see the sidebar "The Gap Between Communication and Intent.")

THE GAP BETWEEN COMMUNICATION AND INTENT

One of the most common occurrences in stressful conversations is that we all start relying far too much on our intentions. As the mercury in the emotional thermometer rises, we presume that other people automatically understand what we mean. We assume, for instance, that people know we mean well. Indeed, research shows that in stressful conversations, most speakers assume that the listener believes that they have good intentions, regardless of what they say.

Intentions can never be that powerful in communications—and certainly not in stressful conversations.

To see what I mean, just think of the last time someone told you not to take something the wrong way. This may well have been uttered quite sincerely by the speaker; nevertheless, most people automatically react by stiffening inwardly, anticipating something at least mildly offensive or antagonistic. And that is exactly the reaction that phrase is always going to get. Because the simplest rule about stressful conversations is that people don't register intention *despite* words; we register intention *through* words. In stressful conversations in particular, the emphasis is on what is actually said, not on what we intend or feel. This doesn't mean that participants in stressful conversations don't have feelings or intentions that are valid and valuable. They do. But when we talk

(Continued)

41

THE GAP BETWEEN COMMUNICATION AND INTENT

about people in stressful communication, we're talking about communication between people—and not about intentions.

Of course, in difficult conversations we may all wish that we didn't have to be so explicit. We may want the other person to realize what we mean even if we don't spell it out. But that leads to the wrong division of labor: with the listener interpreting rather than the speaker communicating. In all conversations, but especially in stressful ones, we are all responsible for getting across to one another precisely what we want to say. In the end, it's far more dignified for an executive to come right out and tell an employee, "Corey, I've arranged for you to speak with HR, because you won't be with us after the end of July." Forcing someone to guess your intentions only prolongs the agony of the inevitable.

This technique will work for Elizabeth regardless of Rafael's motive. If Rafael innocently misunderstood what she was saying, she isn't fighting him. She accepts his take on what she said and did and corrects it. If his motive is hostile, Elizabeth doesn't concur just to appease him. She accepts and retries. No one loses face. No one scores points off the other. No one gets drawn off on a tangent.

Fight tactics, not people

Rafael may have baffled Elizabeth, but Karen was acting with outright malice toward Nick when she flew off the handle after a disastrous meeting with the client. Nick certainly can't prevent her from using the thwarting tactics with which she has been so successful in the past. But he can separate Karen's character from her behavior. For instance, it's much more useful for him to think of Karen's reactions as thwarting tactics rather than as personal characteristics. If he thinks of Karen as a distorting, hostile, threatening person, where does that lead? What can anyone ever do about another person's character? But if Nick sees Karen's behavior as a series of tactics that she is using with him because they have worked for her in the past, he can think about using countering techniques to neutralize them.

The best way to neutralize a tactic is to name it. It's much harder to use a tactic once it is openly identified. If Nick, for instance, had said, "Karen, we've worked together pretty well for a long time. I don't know how to talk about what went wrong in the meeting when your take on what happened, and what's going on now, is so different from mine," he would have changed the game completely. He neither would have attacked Karen nor remained the pawn of her tactics. But he would have made Karen's tactics in the conversation the dominant problem.

Openly identifying a tactic, particularly an aggressive one, is disarming for another reason. Often we think of an aggressive counterpart as persistently, even endlessly, contentious, but that isn't true. People have definite levels of aggression that they're comfortable with—and they are reluctant to raise the bar. When Nick doesn't acknowledge Karen's tactics, she can use them unwittingly, or allegedly so. But if Nick speaks of them, it would require more aggression on Karen's part to continue using the same tactics. If she is at or near her aggression threshold, she won't continue because that would make her uncomfortable. Nick may not be able to stop Karen, but she may stop herself.

People think stressful conversations are inevitable. And they are. But that doesn't mean they have to have bad resolutions. Consider a client of mine, Jacqueline, the only woman on the board of an engineering company. Another board member repeatedly ribbed her about being a feminist and, on this occasion, he was telling a sexist joke.

This wasn't the first time that something like this had happened, and Jacqueline felt the usual internal cacophony of reactions. But because she was aware that this was a stressful situation for her, Jacqueline was prepared. First, she let the joke hang in the air for a minute and then went back to the issue they had been discussing. When Richard didn't let it go but escalated with a new poke—"Come on, Jackie, it was a *joke*"—Jacqueline stood her ground. "Richard," she said, "this kind of humor is frivolous to you, but it is wrong, and moreover, it makes me, the only woman on this board, feel pushed aside." Jacqueline didn't need to say more. If Richard had continued to escalate, he would have lost face. In fact, he backed down: "Well, I wouldn't want my wife to hear about my bad behavior a second time," he snickered. Jacqueline was silent. She had made her point; there was no need to take it further.

Stressful conversations are never easy, but we can all fare better if, like Jacqueline, we prepare for them by developing greater awareness of our vulnerabilities and better techniques for handling ourselves.

The advice and tools described in this article can be helpful in unilaterally reducing the strain in stressful conversations. All you have to do is try them. If one technique doesn't work, try another. Find phrasing that feels natural. But keep practicing—you'll find what works best for you.

HOLLY WEEKS publishes, teaches, and consults on communications issues. She is an adjunct lecturer in public policy at the Harvard Kennedy School and the author of *Failure to Communicate: How Conversations Go Wrong and What You Can Do to Right Them* (Harvard Business Review Press, 2008).

Adapted from an article in *Harvard Business Review*, July–August 2001 (product #R0107H).

3

The Secret to Dealing with Difficult People: It's About You

By Tony Schwartz

D o you have someone at work who consistently triggers you? Doesn't listen? Takes credit for work you've done? Wastes your time with trivial issues? Acts like a know-it-all? Can only talk about himself? Constantly criticizes?

Our core emotional need is to feel valued and valuable. When we don't, it's deeply unsettling, a challenge to our sense of equilibrium, security, and well-being. At the most primal level, it can feel like a threat to our very survival.

This is especially true when the person you're struggling with is your boss. The problem is that being in charge of other people rarely brings out the best in us.

"Power tends to corrupt, and absolute power corrupts absolutely," Lord Acton said way back in 1887. "There is no worse heresy than the office that sanctifies the holder of it."

The easy default when we feel devalued is to play the role of victim, and it's a seductive pull. Blaming others for how we're feeling is a form of self-protection. Whatever is going wrong isn't our fault. By off-loading responsibility, we feel better in the short term.

The problem with being a victim is that you cede the power to influence your circumstances. The painful truth when it comes to the people who trigger you is this: You're not going to change them. The only person you have the possibility of changing is yourself.

Each of us has a default lens through which we see the world. We call it reality, but in fact it's a selective filter. We have the power to view the world through other lenses. There are three worth trying on when you find yourself defaulting to negative emotions.

The lens of realistic optimism. Using this lens requires asking yourself two simple questions when you feel you're being treated badly or unfairly. The first one is, "What are the facts in this situation?" The second is, "What's the story I'm telling myself about those facts?"

Making this distinction allows you to stand outside your experience rather than simply reacting to it. It also opens the possibility that whatever story you're currently telling yourself isn't necessarily the only way to look at your situation.

Realistic optimism, a term coined by the psychologist Sandra Schneider, means telling yourself the most hopeful and empowering story about a given circumstance without subverting the facts. It's about moving beyond your default reaction to feel under attack and exploring whether there is an alternative way of viewing the situation that would ultimately serve you better. Another way of discovering an alternative is to ask yourself, "How would I act here at my best?"

The reverse lens. This lens requires viewing the world through the lens of the person who triggered you. It doesn't mean sacrificing your own point of view but rather widening your perspective.

It's nearly certain that the person you perceive as difficult views the situation differently than you do. With the reverse lens, you ask yourself, "What is this person feeling, and in what ways does that make sense?" Or put more starkly: "Where's my responsibility in all this?"

Counterintuitively, one of the most powerful ways to reclaim your value, when it feels threatened, is to find a way to appreciate the perspective of the person you feel devalued by. It's called empathy.

Just as you do, others tend to behave better when they feel seen and valued—especially since insecurity is what usually prompts them to act badly in the first place.

The long lens. Sometimes your worst fears about another person turn out to be true. He is someone who bullies you unreasonably, and seeing it from his perspective doesn't help. She does invariably take credit for your work.

When your current circumstances are incontrovertibly bad, the long lens provides a way of looking beyond the present to imagine a better future. Begin with this question: "Regardless of how I feel about what's happening right now, how can I grow and learn from this experience?" How many times has something that felt terrible to you in the moment turned out to be trivial several months later or actually led you to an important opportunity or in a positive new direction?

My last boss fired me. It felt awful at the time, but it also pushed me way out of my comfort zone, which is where it turned out I needed to go.

Looking back, the story I tell myself is that for all his deficiencies, I learned a lot from that boss, and it all serves me well today. I can understand, from his point of view, why he found me difficult as an employee, without feeling devalued. Most important, getting fired prompted me to make a decision—founding the company I now run—that has brought me more happiness than any other work I've ever done.

TONY SCHWARTZ is the president and CEO of The Energy Project and the author of *Be Excellent at Anything* (Free-Press, 2011). Become a fan of The Energy Project on Facebook and connect with Tony on Twitter at @TonySchwartz and @Energy_Project.

Reprinted from hbr.org, originally published October 12, 2011.

4

How to Deal with a Mean Colleague

By Amy Gallo

When a colleague is mean to you, it can be hard to know how to respond. Some people are tempted to let aggressive behavior slide in the hopes that the person will stop. Others find themselves fighting back. When you're being treated poorly by a coworker, how can you change the dynamic? And if the behavior persists or worsens, how do you know when you're dealing with a true bully?

What the experts say

"When it comes to bad behavior at work, there's a broad spectrum," with outright bullies on one end and people who are simply rude on the other, says Michele Woodward, an executive coach and host of HBR's webinar "Bullies, Jerks, and Other Annoyances: Identify and Defuse the Difficult People at Work." You may not know which end of the spectrum you're dealing with until you actually address the behavior. If it's a bully, it can be difficult—if not impossible—to get the person to change, says Gary Namie, founder of the Workplace Bullying Institute and author of *The Bully at Work*. But in most cases, you can—and should—take action. "Know that you have a solution, you're not powerless," says Woodward. Here are some tactics to consider when dealing with an aggressive colleague.

Understand why

The first step is to understand what's causing the behavior. Research from Nathanael Fast, an assistant professor at the University of Southern California's

Marshall School of Business, proves a commonly held idea: People act out when their ego is threatened. "We often see powerful people behave aggressively toward less powerful people when their competence is questioned," he says. Namie agrees: "People who are skilled and well-liked are the most frequent targets precisely because they pose a threat." So it may help to stroke the aggressor's ego. "In our study, we saw that if the subordinate offered gratitude to the boss, it wiped out the effect," Fast explains. Even a small gesture, such as ending an email with "Thanks so much for your help" or complimenting the person on something you genuinely admire, can help.[1]

Look at what you're doing

These situations also require introspection. "It's very easy to say, 'Oh, that person is a jerk,'" Woodward says. But perhaps you work in a highly competitive culture or one that doesn't prioritize politeness. Consider whether you might be misinterpreting the behavior or overreacting to it or whether you've unknowingly contributed to the problem. Have you in any way caused the person to feel threatened or to see you as disloyal? Self-evaluation can be tough, so get a second opinion from someone you trust, who will tell you the truth, not just what you want to hear. Don't put too much of the blame on yourself, however. "It's important to balance not being threatening with not being a doormat, which just invites more aggression," Fast says. "Targets regularly assume it's their fault," when it's not, Namie agrees.

Stand up for yourself

Don't be afraid to call out the bad behavior when it happens. "I believe very strongly in making immediate corrections," says Woodward. "If someone calls you 'Honey' in a meeting, say right then: 'I don't like being called that. Please use my name,'" she says. If you're uncomfortable with an immediate, public response, Woodward advises saying something as soon as you're able. After the meeting, you could say, "I didn't like being called 'Honey.' It demeans me." Show that there is no reward for treating you that way. "The message should be: Don't mess with me; it won't be worth your effort," Namie says.

Enlist help

"Everybody should have alliances at work—peers and people above and below, who can be your advocates and champions," says Woodward. Talk to those supporters and see what they can do to help, whether it's simply confirming your perspective or speaking on your behalf. Of course, you may need to escalate the situation to someone more senior or to HR. But before that, "you owe it to the relationship to try to solve it informally," says Woodward.

Demonstrate the cost to the business

If you do need to take formal action, start with your boss (assuming he isn't the aggressor). But you may need to take the issue higher up the hierarchy. When you have someone's ear, Namie recommends focusing the conversation on how the person's behavior is hurting the business. "Talk about how it's affecting morale and performance," says Fast. Personal pleas rarely work and too often degenerate into he said-she said type arguments. "Don't tell a story of emotional wounds," Namie advises. "Make an argument that the person is costing the organization money."

Know the limitations

When none of the above works you have to consider: Is this uncivil, mean behavior, or am I being bullied? If you are in an abusive situation (not just a tough one), Namie and Woodward agree that chances of change are low. "The only time I've seen a bully change is when they are publicly fired. Sanctions don't work," says Woodward. Instead, you need to take action to protect yourself. Of course, in an ideal world, senior leaders would immediately fire people who are toxic to a workplace. But both Namie and Woodward agree that it rarely happens. "Even though the statistics are clear on the impact [of bullying] on morale, retention, and performance, it's very hard for organizations to take action," Woodward says. If you're in an abusive situation at work, the most tenable solution may be to leave—if that's a possibility. The Workplace Bullying Institute has done online surveys that show more people stay in a bullying situation because of pride (40% of respondents) than because of economics (38%). If you're worried about letting the bully win, Namie says, you're better off worrying about your own well-being.[3]

Principles to remember

Do:

- Know that most people act aggressively at work because they feel threatened.

- Ask yourself whether you're being overly sensitive or misinterpreting the situation.

- Call out the inappropriate behavior in the moment.

Don't:

- Take the blame. Many bullies pick targets that are highly skilled and well-liked.

- Escalate the situation until you've tried to solve it informally and with the help of your allies.

- Suffer unnecessarily. If the situation persists and you can leave, do it.

Case study #1: Don't stay and suffer

Eleven years ago Heather Reynolds took a new position at a veterinary clinic owned by another veterinarian named Adam with the intention of buying into the practice (names and details in these case studies have been changed). At first, Adam seemed thrilled about Heather coming to work with him. "He was positive, supportive, and encouraging. He was over the moon about me joining," she says. After several months, she bought half of the firm and became Adam's business partner.

Things continued to go well until a year later when, after what seemed like a minor disagreement, Adam stopped speaking to Heather for six weeks. When she confronted him, he told her he was considering dropping her as a partner. Heather was shocked. She had taken out a loan to buy into the firm and felt stuck.

Eventually they got back on track, but Heather soon learned that this was a pattern of behavior. Any time there was conflict, Adam reacted the same way. "If I disagreed, he would ice me out. If I confronted him, he'd ice me out longer," she says. She eventually figured out that stroking his ego was more effective. "You could flatter him, tell him how great he was, how he did well in a case, and he'd be back on your side. I learned to do this sort of dance in order to survive."

But Adam's harsh behavior took its toll on Heather. Last year, things got so bad that he didn't speak to her for three months. Heather sought the advice of a professional coach, who helped her see that Adam was a narcissist and a bully who was threatened by her skills. Late last year, she told him she was looking for someone to buy out her part of the business and he offered to do it. "It was the best thing I could've done," she says. "I wished I'd left when he first showed me who he truly was."

Case study #2: Call out the bad behavior

Christine Johnson was excited about her new role as deputy editor at a San Francisco–based media company. The position had just been created, so she would be managing a team of existing staff, and everyone welcomed her except for one person, Terry. "What I didn't know and I learned later was that he wanted the role and was angry that he didn't get it," she says.

During her first weeks on the job, Terry was aggressive. "I was constantly fending off little attacks from him," she remembers. He kept asking her how she wanted to supervise their work, what processes she wanted to put in place, how he should interact with her about his projects. Looking back, Heather realizes these were all questions designed to make her look unprepared and incompetent. "And I was too green to say I didn't know yet," she says.

Terry started sending Christine 50 emails with return receipt before 9:00 a.m. When she hadn't responded by 11:00 a.m., he would start emailing her to ask if she'd seen his emails. "He was constantly badgering me. I actually considered quitting. I didn't feel like I had any allies and wasn't sure this was the job I wanted," she says. After five weeks of this abuse, Christine stood up to Terry in a staff meeting. "He kept asking me questions over and over, and I just lost my cool," she says. She snapped at Terry and said, "I'm sick of you asking me so many unnecessary questions. Can you please stop?" Terry backed down

Christine was embarrassed by her behavior, but later, when she was in her office, people began stopping by to thank her for standing up to Terry. "Once I had a small amount of reinforcement from my peers, I knew I could take him on," she says. And once he saw that she wasn't willing to take his abuse, he stood down. "It got better and we were cordial, but it was an awful start," she says.

AMY GALLO is a contributing editor at *Harvard Business Review* and the author of the *HBR Guide to Dealing with Conflict* (Harvard Business Review Press, 2017). She writes and speaks about workplace dynamics. See her website amyegallo .com and follow her on Twitter @amyegallo.

Notes

1. N. J. Fast and S. Chen, "When the Boss Feels Inadequate: Power, Incompetence, and Aggression," *Psychological Science* 20, no. 11 (November 2009): 1406–1413; and "A Simple 'Thanks' Can Tame the Barking Boss," *Psychological Science*, October 30, 2013, http://www.psychological science.org/index.php/news/minds-business/a-simple -thanks-can-tamc-the-barking-boss.html.
2. G. Namie, "2014 WBI U.S. Workplace Bullying Survey," Workplace Bullying Institute, February 2014, http://www .workplacebullying.org/wbiresearch/wbi-2014-us-survey/.

Adapted from content posted on hbr.org,
October 16, 2014 (product #H011T2).

5

How to Deal with a Passive-Aggressive Colleague

By Amy Gallo

Your colleague says one thing in a meeting but then does another. He passes you in the hallway without saying hello and talks over you in meetings. But when you ask to speak with him about his behavior, he insists that everything's fine and the problem is all in your head. But it's not: He's being passive-aggressive. Working with someone like this can be so frustrating. Do you address the behavior directly? Or try to ignore it? How can you get to the core issue when your colleague pretends that nothing's going on?

What the experts say

It's not uncommon for colleagues to occasionally make passive-aggressive remarks to one another over particularly sensitive issues or when they feel they can't be direct. "We're all guilty of doing it once in a while," says Amy Su, coauthor of *Own the Room: Discover Your Signature Voice to Master Your Leadership Presence*. But persistent passive-aggressive behavior is a different ballgame. "These are people who will often do anything to get what they need, including lie," says Annie McKee, founder of the Teleos Leadership Institute and coauthor of *Primal Leadership: Unleashing the Power of Emotional Intelligence*. In these cases, you have to take special precautions that help you, and hopefully your counterpart, both get your jobs done. Here are some tips.

Don't get caught up

When your coworker pretends nothing is going on or accuses you of overreacting, it's hard not to get angry and defensive. But "this is not one of those situations to fight fire with fire," McKee says. Do your best to remain calm. "The person may want you to get mad so they can then blame you, which is a release of their own anxiety," Su explains. "Responding in an emotional way will likely leave you looking—and feeling—like the fool. This is your opportunity to be the bigger person."

Consider what's motivating the behavior

People who routinely act in a passive-aggressive way aren't necessarily complete jerks. It could be that they don't know how to communicate or are afraid of conflict. McKee says that passive-aggressive behavior is often a way for people to "get their emotional point across without having true, healthy conflict." There's also a self-centeredness to it. "They make the flawed assumption that others should know what they're feeling and that their needs and preferences are more important than [those of] others," says Su. Understand this, but don't try to diagnose all your colleague's problems. "You just have to see it for what it is," Su adds: "an unproductive expression of emotions that they can't share constructively."

Own your part

Chances are that you're not blameless in the situation. Ask yourself if something you're doing is contributing to the dynamic or causing the person to be passive-aggressive. "Own your half," says Su. Also, consider whether you've dished out the same behavior; know the signs.[1] "It can happen to even the best of us, whether we're procrastinating or wanting to avoid something. We might leak emotions in a way that's hurtful to others," says Su.

Focus on the content, not the delivery

It might be the last thing you want to do, but try to see the situation from your colleague's perspective. What is the underlying opinion or perspective she's attempting to convey with her snarky comment? "Analyze the position the person is trying to share with you," says McKee. Does she think that the way you're running the project isn't working? Or does she disagree about your team goals? "Not everyone knows how to publicly discuss or express what they think," says Su. If you can focus on the underlying business concern or question rather than the way she's expressing herself, you can move on to addressing the actual problem.

Acknowledge the underlying issue

Once you're calm and able to engage in a productive conversation, go back to the person. Say something like, "You made a good point in that exchange we had the other day. Here's what I heard you saying." This will help them talk about the substance of their concerns." By joining *with* them, you'll have a better chance of turning the energy around," McKee explains. Do this in a matter-of-fact way, without discussing how the sentiment was expressed. "Don't listen or give any credence to the toxic part," advises Su. "Sometimes it's that they just want their opinion heard."

Watch your language

Whatever you say, don't accuse the person of being passive-aggressive. "That can hurt your cause," says McKee. Su agrees: "It's such a loaded word. It would put someone who's already on the defensive into a more angry position. Don't label or judge them." Instead, McKee suggests recounting how some of your previous interactions have played out and explaining the impact it's having on you and possibly others. If feasible, show that the behavior is working against something your counterpart cares about, like achieving the team's goals.

Find safety in numbers

You don't have to deal with this situation alone. "It's OK to reality check with others and have allies in place to say you're not crazy," says Su. But be sure to frame your discussions as an attempt to constructively improve the relationship, so it doesn't come across as gossiping or bad-mouthing your colleague. Su suggests you ask for honest opinions, something like "I was wondering how Emily's comment landed with you. How did you interpret that?"

Set guidelines for everyone

You might also enlist the help of others in coming up with a long-term solution. "As a team, you can build healthy norms," McKee says. Together you can agree to be more up-front about frustrations and model the honest and direct interactions you want to happen. You can also keep one another accountable. If your problematic colleague tends to ignore agreements, you might take notes in meetings about who's supposed to do what by when, so there are clear action items. The worst offenders are likely to give in to the positive peer pressure and public accountability.

Get help in extreme situations

When a colleague persistently tries to undermine you or prevent you from doing your job and outside observers confirm your take on the situation, you might have to go further. "If you share the same manager, you may be able to ask for help," says McKee. You might tell your boss, "A lot of us have noticed a particular behavior, and I want to talk about how it's impacting my ability to do my work." But "step into those waters carefully," she warns. "Your manager may be hoodwinked by the person and may not see the same behaviors or be conflict averse himself and not want to see it."

Protect yourself

"If there's an interdependence in your work, make sure you're meeting your commitments and deadlines," Su says. "Copy others on important emails. Don't let that person speak for you or represent you in meetings. After a meeting, document agreements and next steps." McKee also suggests keeping records. "Track specific behaviors so that you have examples if needed," she says. "It's hard to argue with the facts." She also recommends you try to avoid working with the person and "keep contact to a minimum. If you have to work together, do it in a group setting" where your colleague is likely to be on better behavior. You might not be able to break the person of his passive-aggressive habits, but you can control your reaction to it.

Principles to remember

Do:

- Understand why people typically act this way: Their needs probably aren't being met.

- Focus on the message your colleague is trying to convey, even if their delivery is misguided.

- Take a step back and ask yourself if you're contributing to the issue in some way.

Don't:

- Lose your cool. Address the underlying business issue in a calm, matter-of-fact way.

- Accuse the person of acting passive-aggressively—that will only make them madder.

- Assume you can change your colleague's behavior.

Case study #1: Make your coworker publicly accountable

One of Mitch Davis's coworkers in the student guidance office of the public high school where he worked was making things difficult for him (names and details in both these case studies have been changed). "She would agree to a plan in a meeting but then sabotage it by not following through," he explains. His colleague, Sarah, defended herself by saying things like "That's not how I remember it" or "I didn't think we had finalized the plan." He tried to talk about these "misunderstandings" with her, but she always shrugged him off. "She'd say she was busy or didn't have time to talk," he explained.

When Mitch told Jim, his and Sarah's boss, that a certain project hadn't gotten done because of this strange dynamic, Jim said that he had noticed the pattern too. Together, they devised a plan to make Sarah more accountable. "He and I agreed that he would publicly ask for a volunteer to take notes on each meeting, [documenting] who would be responsible for accomplishing each task and by when," Mitch recalls. He was the first volunteer.

And the approach worked. After Mitch sent around the task list, Sarah couldn't make excuses. She was accountable to everyone who attended the meetings. And Mitch didn't mind the additional work: "The extra effort I put in was less than the time I was spending fuming about my coworker and running around to pick up the pieces of the things she didn't complete. It actually helped everyone in our department be more productive and was something we should have done a long time ago."

Case study #2: Get help sooner rather than later

Emily Sullivan, a digital marketing consultant at a small agency, had recently been promoted and managed an eight-person team. One of her direct reports, Will, had only been at the agency for three months before Emily's promotion, and he clearly wasn't thrilled to suddenly have her as a new boss. But "he was a top performer and extremely competent," Emily recalls, and since they'd worked "fairly harmoniously together as colleagues," she was happy to have him in the group.

Unfortunately, Will became very difficult to manage. He didn't communicate with Emily unless absolutely necessary, he didn't actively engage in training sessions that she offered, and he "poked holes" in her initiatives. "He took every opportunity to make it clear that he didn't value my input," she explains.

Surprised and dismayed by his attitude, Emily decided to address it as she would with any other team member: directly and clearly. She started by asking him in their one-on-one meetings whether something was wrong. He said there wasn't, but the behavior persisted, so she tried taking him out for coffee and asking whether she had unknowingly offended him or if he wanted to be managed in a different way. He acknowledged that there was a "personality clash," but he ended the conversation there and continued to treat her dismissively at the office. She heard from other staff members that he had even called her "lazy and useless."

"The last thing I wanted was to pass the issue further up the chain and potentially harm Will's career," she says. After all, he was a valuable team member, and she wanted to protect him. But she came to see that she should have gone to her manager from the start. When she eventually did, her boss pointed out that her failure to effectively manage a key team member amounted to poor performance on her part.

Within a year both Emily and Will voluntarily left the agency, but neither was happy with the circumstances. She says that if she could do it over again she would've talked to her manager sooner, kept better records on Will's "toxic attitude," and, when there weren't drastic improvements, fired him "without hesitation."

AMY GALLO is a contributing editor at *Harvard Business Review* and the author of the *HBR Guide to Dealing with Conflict* (Harvard Business Review Press, 2017). She writes and speaks about workplace dynamics. See her website amyegallo .com and follow her on Twitter @amyegallo.

Note

1. See, for example, Muriel Maignan Wilkins, "Signs You're Being Passive-Aggressive," hbr.org, June 20, 2014, https:// hbr.org/2014/06/signs-youre-being-passive-aggressive/.

Adapted from content posted on hbr.org,
January 11, 2016 (product #H02LQP).

6

How to Work with Someone Who's Always Stressed Out

By Rebecca Knight

We all know people who seem to be constantly stressed out—who claim to be buried in work, overloaded with projects, and without a minute to spare. Colleagues like that can be difficult to work with, but you probably don't have a choice. How do you deal with coworkers who can't handle stress? Should you address the issue directly? Or try other tactics to help them calm down and focus? And how can you protect yourself from their toxic emotions?

What the experts say

Stress is part of everyday life. "We all go through periods when we are dealing with a lot of stress," says Caroline Webb, author of *How to Have a Good Day*. "Those periods might last 10 minutes, 10 days, or 10 months." But for certain people, "stress is a habitual pattern." These folks always "feel overwhelmed, constantly stretched, and always out of their depth." Working closely with a person like this can be a real challenge. "But you mustn't make them the villain," says Holly Weeks, author of *Failure to Communicate*. "Don't think, *What can I do to change this person?* Think about how to neutralize the situation and what you can do for yourself." Whether you regard your colleague with annoyance or sympathy, here are some tips on how to collaborate more effectively.

Don't judge

First things first: Check that you're not being too judgmental. "There's an enormous range in people's tolerance level for stress, and stress that may feel toxic to you may be stimulating to someone else," Weeks explains. "So unless you're a psychologist, judging someone's way of handling stress as inappropriate is fraught." Try to think of your colleague's disposition "as not a character flaw but a characteristic." Webb notes that your coworker may just be responding to the "always-on nature of work" nowadays. "There was a time when we could go home and forget about work until the next day," but the modern era's "pressure to stay connected" weighs on some more than others.

Acknowledge the stress

It's important to make the stressed-out person feel "seen and heard," Webb says. "Say something like,

'I notice you were working late last night, and it wasn't the first time. How are things going?'" Then, after your colleague recites the usual catalog of pressures, "say, 'That must be hard.' It doesn't matter if you believe it or not. That's how this person is feeling. Acknowledging it gives you both a chance to move beyond." At the same time, Weeks says, you mustn't "enable" or agitate your colleague by making comments like, "I don't know how you can you stand it! This company is working you to death!" That's not helpful. Instead, she says, say something more neutral, like "You have a lot of balls in the air."

Offer praise

One of the best ways to "get a stressed person out of fight-or-flight mode [is to] pay a compliment," Webb says. "This person is feeling out of control, incompetent, and disrespected. A compliment is your easy way to help them get back to their better self." Praising someone's performance in the workplace gives the person an alternative "self-image of being a competent, positive professional," Weeks adds. Cite something specific. For instance, you could say, "The way you handled that presentation last week was admirable. You were so calm and collected and the clients were impressed." Appreciation can be a powerful intervention. "When you tell people how you see them, they step into that role."

Offer your assistance

Another strategy is to offer your support. "Say, 'Is there anything that I, or anyone on my team, can do to help to you?'" Webb suggests. "Chances are that you can't do anything, but your offer will give the other person a chance to think about solutions and feel that he's not out on his own." Be clear, however, that this isn't a blanket invitation to be used anytime, anywhere, Weeks says. "Give caveats about what you're able to do." The message should be, "I'm a limited resource, but I want to help you if you are in a pickle."

Break down your requests

When dealing with stressed-out colleagues, think about ways to "reduce their cognitive load," Webb says. "Don't add to their sense of being overwhelmed." You might, for instance, shorten your emails to the person, split your larger requests into several smaller steps, or encourage the idea of dividing work into manageable chunks. "Be smart about how you break down your ask," she adds. But don't go too far. You'll have to reconcile your colleague's deficiencies with your own desire and need to complete tasks. After all, "your job is to get done what you need to get done."

Ask for a read

If your coworker's anxieties seem to be having an impact on their ability to focus—and you're genuinely worried about their health—ask them to provide more detail, Weeks recommends. "Say, 'On a scale of 1 to 10, how worried should I be about your level of stress?' Signal that you can't read how bad it is for them." The answers may surprise you. "They may tell you, 'Oh, this is a 5,' in which case you don't need to call an ambulance. Or they may reveal that their wife has cancer and they're going through something very hard." To a large degree, the roots of the tension "are none of your business."

Get some distance

Stress can be contagious, so "have the self-awareness to know the effect it's having on you," Webb says. "When someone is toxic and draining your energy, you sometimes have to figure out how you can get distance from that person or limit your interactions with them." Of course, this isn't always easy—particularly if you work in the same department and are assigned to the same projects. In that case, Weeks says, look at the bright side of the situation. "When it comes to office characters, the laconic, laid-back, doesn't-carry-their-weight type is the person who's going to leave you in a jam," she explains. "While you may not prefer the stress case's temperament, it's less of a problem."

Principles to remember

Do:

- Offer support by asking if there's anything you can do to help. This will help your stressed-out colleague feel less alone.

- Improve your colleague's self-image by offering praise.

- Think about ways to reduce the person's cognitive load by, for instance, breaking work up into more-manageable chunks.

Don't:

- Judge. Your colleague may express stress differently than you, but that's not necessarily a character flaw.

- Enable the person. Simply acknowledge the stress, then try to help your colleague move beyond it.

- Get sucked in. Instead, figure out ways to get distance from your colleague.

Case study #1: Offer your help and perspective

Karoli Hindriks, founder and CEO of Jobbatical, the international job placement firm, previously worked at a company where she supervised a highly anxious marketing executive. The colleague—we'll call her

Jenny—"was so overwhelmed and stressed out by her work that her overall performance was really beginning to suffer," Karoli recalls. "Everyone could see how hard she was working. But I also saw the dark circles under her eyes, her jumpy mood, and her irritability."

Karoli knew that it wasn't her place to judge; Jenny just seemed to be wired that way. Instead, she offered support and talked about the work that Jenny had to do in terms of small steps rather than a single large, daunting task. "I asked her to imagine a messy room that she needed to clean up. I told her to think of stepping into that room and seeing the clothes scattered all over the floor, the mountain of candy wrappers under the bed, and the layer of dust covering every surface."

"I told her she had two options: She could give up, fall apart, and surrender to the mess, or she could pick up the first pair of socks you see and feel good about being one step closer to cleaning up that mess.

Step by step, inch by inch, item by item, she would create order."

Karoli says that message got through to Jenny. "I started to see her sharing more of her small victories and how happy that was making her," she says. "Her performance improved drastically, and her team members felt comfortable communicating with her again."

Case study #2: Be empathetic and praise your stressed-out colleague's strengths

Earlier in her career, Jan Bruce worked as a publisher and editor at a consumer health and wellness magazine. "It was a high-stress environment in a pressure-cooker industry," she recalls. "There were a lot of big personalities strutting around the office. The culture was toxic, and people were inclined to be disparaging."

One of her closest colleagues—we'll call her Abby—became consumed by the strain of her job. "She had been very successful in the organization and had gotten many promotions, so she was under extreme pressure," Jan explains. At a certain point, she started working so hard that "she was unable to focus. The stress was making her sick."

Jan remembers approaching Abby with a "spirit of empathy" and concern. "I said, 'I know that you're under a lot of pressure. How are you coping?' which made Abby want to talk to me and confide in me."

Through subsequent conversations, Jan saw that Abby was determined to achieve and be successful, but she also needed to give herself a break and let some of the stress go. "She had an attitude of, 'I will overcome this. If I just work longer and harder, everything will be okay.'"

Jan responded by complimenting Abby's skills and abilities. "I said, 'You are doing all of this great work, and you've been put in charge of a whole new division, plus you have four small children at home. No matter what you're feeling today, you are enormously smart and competent. You have to remember that. If you ever forget, I'm here to remind you.'"

Abby appreciated the support, and the two ultimately developed a strong working relationship.

Today Jan is the cofounder and CEO of MeQuilibrium, a software platform that helps companies and workers better manage their productivity, health, and well-being.

REBECCA KNIGHT is a freelance journalist in Boston and a lecturer at Wesleyan University. Her work has been published in the *New York Times*, *USA Today*, and the *Financial Times*.

Reprinted from hbr.org, originally published
August 7, 2017 (product #H03TO8).

7

How to Manage Someone Who Thinks Everything Is Urgent

By Liz Kislik

W e've all been in situations where we couldn't wait for a slow-moving or overly cautious employee to take action. But at the other extreme, some employees have such a deep need to get things resolved that they move too quickly, or too intensely, and make a mess. They may make a bad deal just to say they've made it or issue a directive without thinking through the ramifications just to say they've handled a problem decisively.

The problem is that these employees may have been praised in the past for this very behavior, even when it results in mistakes that they can then heroically "save." And when urgency is a part of the organizational culture, it may feel like a requirement to move fast, whether you're a leader or a frontline employee. At a basic level, because urgency generates so much activity, it can be hard to recognize it as an organizational problem. But it's a significant one. Executives report that thousands of dollars are lost every business day when decisions are rote or arbitrary because of pro forma, nonstrategic decision making.

And yet, despite the damage that unaddressed urgency can do, urgent employees are usually some of the most committed and are often very productive. Here are steps you can take to mitigate the negative impact of their urgency, to help them focus their intensity on the right targets, and to ensure they make better long-term decisions before taking action.

Help them recognize their impact on others. Show your urgent employees how collaboration pays off for everyone—including them. One assistant VP I worked with was correct about what needed to be accomplished, but he was driven to get it over with and put it behind him and often operated unilaterally to get things done. Because he was only urgent about his own goals and tasks, he was perceived as a bad partner and not a team player. I encouraged his manager to affirm the importance of collaboration and to ask him to prepare the equivalent of "impact statements" as a way to force interaction and cooperation with other parties. His manager also learned to stop praising him for every accomplishment and to praise him instead for the process: joint planning, coordination, and interdepartmental success.

Encourage them to identify all the consequences of their actions. It's typical for urgent employees to see only the upside of acting quickly, not the negative effects of acting *too* quickly. A VP at a nonprofit client had a history of making decisions hastily and without sufficient data. These decisions led to some unfortunate employee layoffs, even though she had been asked to consult with others and weigh such decisions carefully. After we had her rehearse termination conversations with the employees she had just hired, we dramatized the impact the firings would have on them as individuals and on their families. The exposure to the pain she was causing finally got her attention.

Pair them with long-term thinkers. Effective interventions let urgent employees actually experience the success that comes from a more deliberate, thoughtful approach. A senior sales specialist brought in many deals because he was both diligent and intense. But he was so eager to get the deals that as soon as a prospect indicated even a tentative yes, he would offer anything they seemed to want to close their initial order rather than strengthening his own presentation to get better value. After he brought in several new accounts that were significantly smaller than potential or that had too many strings attached, his management paired him with a more cerebral colleague who excelled in research and planning. The combination of high energy and careful planning increased the number and size of deals.

Coach them to separate urgency from what actually needs to be done. Addressing underlying concerns often mitigates the apparent need for urgency. During a period of organizational growth, a previously solid team leader made people nuts because he seemed to not take others' input, needed to manage everything himself, and didn't share enough information or decision making with his team. His team's growth and development was suppressed, and he was almost always overwhelmed and holding up progress. We discussed various aspects of project management so that he could see he had all the elements under control, and then I asked, "What's the actual pressure?" After some discussion, it became clear that the pressure wasn't from the work itself so much as from feeling alone with the awesome responsibility of handling it all. We used mindfulness techniques to help him cope with the feeling and various other techniques for engaging his team so that they understood the ramifications, how to anticipate, how to shoulder more responsibility, and how to warn him if anything was going off course.

Employees who are driven by excessive urgency often act like they're scratching an itch rather than making intentional efforts to accomplish and grow as much as they can, either for themselves or their organizations. Once they realize that additional reflection and deliberation can generate significantly better results, they can learn to corral their urgency in service of being a better leader and achieving better performance.

LIZ KISLIK has helped organizations from the *Fortune* 500 to national nonprofits and family-run businesses—such as American Express, the American Red Cross, Staples, and Highlights for Children—solve their biggest challenges in organizational performance, talent management, and leadership development while strengthening their top and bottom lines in the process. She has served as adjunct faculty at Hofstra University and New York University, and speaks frequently on the topics of collaboration, managing teams, developing leaders, and improving customer loyalty.

Reprinted from hbr.org, originally published
August 2, 2017 (product #H03TJ0).

8

Do You Hate Your Boss?

By Manfred F. R. Kets de Vries

Stacey really loved her job at a top tech company—that is, until her boss left for another firm. The new manager, Peter, seemed to dislike pretty much everyone on the team he had inherited, regardless of individual or collective performance. He was aloof, prone to micromanaging, and apt to write off any project that wasn't his brainchild. Within a year he had replaced a number of Stacey's colleagues.

At first Stacey (whose name, like others in this article, has been changed to protect her confidentiality) tried to win her new boss's trust and respect by asking for his feedback and guidance. But Peter was unresponsive. Despite her best efforts, Stacey couldn't make the relationship click. When, several months in, she finally decided to approach HR about the problem, she got nothing more than sympathy. The firm was not willing to sanction Peter, because his unit's performance had not materially deteriorated and no one else had lodged a complaint.

Unable to escape or change the dynamic with Peter, Stacey felt stressed, depressed, and increasingly unable to do good work. She worried that the only way out was to leave the company she loved.

Stacey's situation is not uncommon. According to the most recent Gallup State of the Global Workplace study, half of all employees in the United States have quit jobs at some point in their career in order to get away from their bosses. The figures are similar or even higher for workers in Europe, Asia, the Middle East, and Africa.[1]

The same survey, consistent with previous ones, also shows a clear correlation between an employee's engagement (that is, motivation and effort to achieve organizational goals) and his or her relationship with the boss. While 77% of employees who said they were engaged at work described interactions with their managers in positive terms (for example, "my supervisor focuses on my strengths"), only 23% of those who were "not engaged" and a mere 4% of those who were "actively disengaged" did the same. This is worrying, because research has shown that an engaged workforce is a key driver of organizational success. And yet according to Gallup, only 13% of employees worldwide fall into that category.

What are the "bad" bosses doing? Frequently cited grievances include micromanaging, bullying, avoiding conflict, ducking decisions, stealing credit, shifting blame, hoarding information, failing to listen, setting a poor example, slacking, and not developing staff. Such dysfunctional behavior would make anyone unhappy and unproductive. However, whatever sins your boss commits, managing your relationship with them is a critical part of your job. Doing it well is a key indicator of how effective you are.

In my work as a researcher, management coach, and psychoanalyst, I have spent many decades working with senior and high-potential executives to help them resolve dysfunctional dynamics with their managers. This article explores the options available to anyone in the same predicament. Much of it will feel like common sense. But I have found that people often forget that it's in their power to improve bad situations, so having the options systematically laid out can be very helpful.

Practice empathy

The first step is to consider the external pressures your manager is under. Remember, most bad bosses are not inherently bad people; they're good people with weaknesses that can be exacerbated by the pressure to lead and deliver results. So it's important to consider not just how they act but why they're acting that way.

Research has shown time and again that practicing empathy can be a game changer in difficult boss-subordinate relationships and not just as a top-down phenomenon. Experts such as Stephen Covey and Daniel Goleman emphasize the importance of using this key aspect of emotional intelligence to manage up. Neuroscience also suggests that it's an effective strategy, since mirror neurons in the human brain naturally prompt people to reciprocate behaviors. Bottom line: If you work on empathizing with your boss, chances are they will start empathizing with you, and that will benefit everyone.

It may seem difficult to feel for a manager who isn't giving you what you need or whom you actively dislike. But as Goleman showed years ago, empathy can be learned. And recent research from other scholars, including experts at the Menninger Clinic, suggests that if you practice empathy consciously, your perceptions of others' feelings will be more accurate.[2]

I recall the case of George, a sales manager in a big U.S. firm, who had been going out of his way to please his boss, Abby—to no avail. George was extremely frustrated by Abby's lack of attention and support until a colleague told him to imagine being in the boss's shoes. George knew that Abby's own manager was a real taskmaster, famous for setting impossible stretch goals. Once George took that into account, he realized that Abby was not deliberately ignoring him; she simply didn't have time to be supportive, as she was working on several important new business initiatives at once.

Although it may be a conscious exercise, a display of empathy is still best delivered in an informal setting. You don't make an appointment; instead you look for the right moment when the other person will be receptive to your efforts. In George's case it came on a shared business trip to some high-profile accounts in Singapore. Over dinner the first day, he carefully offered Abby an opportunity to open up about the pressures she felt by asking how the new business projects in mainland China were coming along.

Abby turned out to be only too ready to share her stresses and frustrations, and the exchange marked a turning point in what eventually became a very satisfactory working relationship between the two. George worried less about the attention he was (or wasn't) getting, and Abby seemed readier to listen to his problems.

Consider your role

The second step is to look at yourself. In my experience, people who struggle to work well with their bosses are nearly always part of the problem themselves: Their behavior is in some way preventing them from being recognized and valued. This probably isn't what you want to hear, but by acknowledging that you might be doing something wrong, figuring out what it is, and adjusting accordingly, you might be able to salvage the relationship.

Start with some introspection. Consider, as objectively as you can, any criticisms your boss has offered. In what areas do you need to improve? What aspects of your behavior or output might irk him or her?

Also ask yourself what might make your personalities clash. I often find after a fairly short discussion with clients that their managers are "transferential figures," representing authority figures from the past with whom the clients have unresolved issues. Transference of this kind has a powerful influence on behavior and should always be explicitly considered in figuring out dysfunctions in any boss-subordinate relationship.

One client, for example, told me that her boss reminded her of a primary school teacher who had bullied her and whom she had never been able to please. The two resembled each other physically and shared a similar peremptory manner of communicating.

When we surface transference, we can usually take steps to correct for it. After our sessions, my client reported that she found it easier to step back and separate her past resentments from her present reactions and view her boss's comments in a positive light.

Next, observe and seek advice from colleagues who work successfully with your boss. Try to understand the boss's preferences, quirks, and hot buttons, and get some pointers on how you might do things differently. When you approach colleagues, though, make sure to frame any questions carefully. For instance, instead of asking a coworker why the boss always interrupts you when you speak, ask the person, "How do *you* know whether to speak up or not? How can you tell when the boss does or doesn't want input? How do you express disagreement?"

Also take advantage of group training programs to get advice from peers. I remember the case of Tom, who, during a leadership development workshop was asked (like everyone else in his small group) to present an issue that was troubling him. He confessed that he needed to improve his relationship with his boss; whatever he did, it never seemed good enough. His peers were frank in their responses. They said that he often sounded muddled in meetings when trying to explain his business unit goals and that he seemed to be doing a poor job of empowering his direct reports. In the view of his colleagues, this was why the boss was dissatisfied with Tom's performance.

They suggested he spend more time rehearsing and framing his presentations and, in particular, work on proposing less-generic goals and identifying measures of success. They also recommended that he have his subordinates copresent with him and make reports on their own. Tom asked a few clarifying questions and left the workshop eager to apply the advice he'd received. At the next year's planning session, his boss congratulated him on the quality of his group's presentation and followed up with an email praising the teamwork his unit was starting to display.

If feedback from your colleagues doesn't provide any insights into how your behavior might be hurting you, the next step is to try talking to your boss about the problem. Again, approach the conversation delicately, framing your questions in a positive way: "How can I better help you achieve your goals?" rather than "What am I doing wrong?" Position yourself as seeking advice or even mentoring. Request a one-on-one meeting to do this, and give your boss an idea of what you'd like to discuss: performance issues and the development of your management skills.

If you're lucky, he or she will appreciate your willingness to engage and will point out areas to improve, building the foundation for a closer relationship. If your boss stonewalls or rebuffs you, however, that's a clue that the problem isn't you, and you need to figure out what—if anything—you can do to alter things.

Offer a chance to change

If you conclude you're not the one derailing the relationship with your boss, only then should you openly suggest that the two of you don't seem to interact well and that you'd like to remedy the situation.

There are a number of ways into this conversation. If you have the opportunity, you can tack it on as an extension of a frank discussion you're already having. Jeanne, a French executive I once taught, told me about a visit she'd made with her British boss, Richard, to meet a customer. The client gave them both an extremely rough ride, which prompted an exchange between the two of them about what had gone wrong. This gave Jeanne an opening to express some of her frustrations with her boss's behavior, and the two were able to work out how they could improve their own relationship.

If a moment like this does not present itself, you have to initiate the conversation yourself. Most conflict management experts recommend doing that in a private setting where you can't easily be interrupted and where it will be difficult for either of you to leave. To have a constructive talk, it's important that people feel they are in a safe place. Invite your boss out to lunch, perhaps, at a restaurant where you are unlikely to meet colleagues. Explain that you have some private concerns you want to discuss away from the office. If a specific business problem, such as the failure to meet a crucial deadline, came about because of the friction between you, you can say you wish to talk about this event and its implications for other projects—the kind of postmortem that Jeanne and Richard had. Let your boss know to expect a difficult conversation—one that can't be sidestepped. If you just say you want to discuss interpersonal issues, the boss may find some crisis that takes priority.

When you begin a dialogue, you may even discover that your boss is not consciously aware of the degree of your discontent. With Jeanne, for example, one problem was that Richard never asked her for an opinion, listening only to colleagues (also largely British and male) who volunteered their ideas. When they talked about it, Richard explained that he didn't want to put her on the spot in meetings but he had no intention of silencing her.

Organize a mutiny

If you can't improve things by changing your behavior or opening lines of communication with your boss, and if your colleagues feel the same way you do, you should consider alerting HR and the boss's bosses to the problem.

In taking this route, however, you need to make a substantial business case for why your boss is a liability, someone whose poor management will ultimately cause the team's, unit's, or organization's performance to suffer. You must also be prepared to make a credible threat of litigation against the corporation. You'll need documented evidence of the boss's negative impact and inappropriate behavior, such as witness statements and examples of correspondence that clearly breach company rules or HR guidelines. The more people willing to go on record with similar complaints and evidence, the harder it will be for senior managers to ignore or deny the problem.

In the absence of compelling data indicating a pattern of bad behavior, HR representatives are unlikely to be allies; very often they will take the boss's side. Maria, another executive I counseled who had had issues with her boss, initially went to HR for help. But her boss was extremely skilled at self-promotion and persuaded HR that in fact Maria was the problem.

The head of HR not only declined to pursue the matter but even suggested that it was up to Maria to adapt to her boss.

Stories like that are all too common, and many subordinates who have not prepared a strong case against the boss have ended up losing their jobs rather than forcing a change of behavior or practice. Mutiny and whistle-blowing can also damage your future job prospects. Lodging a formal complaint, therefore, should definitely be a last resort.

Play for time or move on

If you are unable to change your relationship with your boss by taking the steps described here, and if there isn't potential for group action, then your options become more limited.

In these situations, most employees simply go through the motions at work and minimize contact with the boss. There is always the possibility, or hope, that he or she will move on. But remember that in playing for time, you also need to set a time limit, so that hanging in doesn't become a way of life. If it does, you will feel disengaged, disenchanted, and even embittered. And that may spill over to other realms, contributing to depression and a range of additional psychosomatic reactions.

The better solution is to look for another job while you're still employed, exiting on your own terms. Beef up your résumé, contact headhunters, line up references, and start interviewing. Having a bad boss isn't your fault, but staying with one will be.

That's ultimately what Stacey concluded. After some soul-searching, she started to hunt for another job. It didn't take her long to find an interesting position in another organization working under a boss with whom she had great rapport. Some months later a former colleague told Stacey that Peter had left the company soon after her. Although his departure was announced as his own choice, the inside scoop was that top management had forced him out because he was losing too many valuable people.

MANFRED F. R. KETS DE VRIES is an executive coach, psychoanalyst, and management scholar. He is the Distinguished Clinical Professor of Leadership Development and Organizational Change at INSEAD in France, Singapore, and Abu Dhabi. His most recent book is *Riding the Leadership Rollercoaster: An Observer's Guide* (Springer, 2017).

Notes

1. "State of the Global Workplace Report 2013," Gallup, http://www.gallup.com/services/178517/state-global -workplace.aspx.
2. J. G. Allen, E. Bleiberg, and T. Haslam-Hopwood, "Understanding Mentalizing: Mentalizing as a Compass for Treatment," Menninger Clinic website, 2003, http:// www.menningerclinic.com/education/clinical-resources/ mentalizing.

Reprinted from *Harvard Business Review*,
December 2016 (product #R1612H).

Index

The most important management ideas all in one place.

We hope you enjoyed this book from *Harvard Business Review*. For the best ideas HBR has to offer turn to HBR's 10 Must Reads Boxed Set. From books on leadership and strategy to managing yourself and others, this 6-book collection delivers articles on the most essential business topics to help you succeed.

HBR's 10 Must Reads Series

The definitive collection of ideas and best practices on our most sought-after topics from the best minds in business.

- Change Management
- Collaboration
- Communication
- Emotional Intelligence
- Innovation
- Leadership
- Making Smart Decisions

- Managing Across Cultures
- Managing People
- Managing Yourself
- Strategic Marketing
- Stratogy
- Teams
- The Essentials

hbr.org/mustreads